T0083731

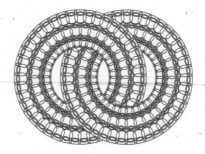

TANTO

TANTO

TANTO TANTO

MARINA CARREIRA

CavanKerry
PRESS

CavanKerry Press Ltd.
Fort Lee, New Jersey
www.cavankerrypress.org

Publisher's Cataloging-In-Publication Data
(Prepared by The Donohue Group, Inc.)
Names: Carreira, Marina, author.
Title: Tanto tanto / Marina Carreira.
Description: First edition. | Fort Lee, New Jersey : CavanKerry Press, 2022.
Identifiers: ISBN 9781933880907
Subjects: LCSH: Lesbianism—Poetry. | Luso Americans—Poetry. |
    Homophobia—Poetry. | Immigrant families—United States—Poetry. |
    LCGFT: Poetry.
Classification: LCC PS3603.A774374 T36 2022 | DDC 811/.6—dc23

Cover artwork: Marina Carreira
Cover and interior text design by Ryan Scheife, Mayfly Design
First Edition 2022, Printed in the United States of America

CAVANKERRY
PRESS

Made possible by funds from the
New Jersey State Council on the Arts, a partner
agency of the National Endowment for the Arts.

CavanKerry Press is grateful for the support it receives
from the New Jersey State Council on the Arts.

In addition, CavanKerry Press gratefully acknowledges generous
emergency support received during the COVID-19 pandemic
from the following funders:

Community of Literary Magazines and Presses

New Jersey Arts and Culture Recovery Fund

New Jersey Council for the Humanities

New Jersey Economic Development Authority

Northern New Jersey Community Foundation

The Poetry Foundation

US Small Business Administration

Also by Marina Carreira

I Sing to That Bird Knowing He Won't Sing Back (2017)
Save the Bathwater (2018)

For Cindy Laura and all queer daughters of immigrants

No one has imagined us.

—Adrienne Rich

Contents

V

Tanto Tanto

Despite the free online chakra test I took in 2013
declaring my heart chakra completely closed and in need

of healing, I'm pretty sure that tuna sandwich you made
me for lunch today opened that bitch right up, at least

stuck a rock at the foot of the door so that all the glorious
light you hold between your teeth filters through, and

fight or flight becomes not so much my mantra but
a little ditty I hum on my way to work in the morning.

You know I'm a sucker for a button-up, so when you come
to me like the most handsome tulip, I'm finally the girl

who got her dream/boat toward the horizon Hurston sang of.
I love you tanto tanto that sometimes the only thing I do

is hold myself together like a woman with too many bags
and not enough groceries, count the minutes till we can flee

to Canada, the hours till our daughters and their bodies
are safe in every space, the day all my chakras align

and I can open
abundantly, astrally, divinely, and *demais*.

I

Baptism

The wispy frost over the brown lawn glistens like a drowsy fawn, greeting the morning, catching the cold with yawn and scowl. I bundle the girls knowing their scarves will unravel, their jackets unzip, their gloves soon prints on the floor of the back seat. We meet other cars trembling with rush hour haste, the red, yellow, and green urban stars urging us to halt, wait, and ride the paths we already know by heart, breath clouds trailing as we enter and exit halls and rooms in what seems like the bluest winter of the longest year. Little do we know.

This rote muscle work of memory works overtime every day but not until it pins me down at dawn. This is to say, before anything happens, I lay wet in my longing for the surge, for my hands surfing the soft dunes of your breasts, your pussy the ocean I swallow whole, this sweet sin our forefathers demand we confess, this church hymn our grandmothers were never allowed to sing. Before the machination of morning, I swell with our light meeting the American gray; in this baptism, I rejoice the doing of things over and over, again and again.

Autobiography of a Fufa

The first time I kissed a girl was after leftover *dobrada* We
    were children
and I didn't worry whether or not she could taste the stomach
    lining still hot
at the back of my tongue All I could think about was how curly
    her hair got
when she sweat, my left foot cramping toes curled so hard at
    the thought
of Avó walking in on us like a tidal wave ripping into
    mid-August

The second time I kissed a girl was in a dream in fourth grade
    about Joana
her lips small but full cool as river water She wore a blue dress
    with daisies on it
and we only tapped real quick because I was nervous and
    knew she didn't know how
to feel seventeen pretty and pregnant by someone else's
    husband She didn't know
if it was a boy or girl just that her father would force an
    abortion

The third time I kissed a girl who called me lezbi in high school
    Her mom
collected Fabergé eggs and always complimented my smile
    She told me to sleep over
Friday so we can go to Abyss for Teen Night We got stupid
    drunk on Fuzzy Navel
and I threw up in her living room and told her mom we had
    some bad seafood while
my leggy friend laughed Sometimes BFFs could kiss you and
    mean nothing by it

The fourth time I kissed a girl I was 23 on my back on a bunny
    slope skis to the sky
and I wanted her to fall in love with me the way Tina and Bette
    did in *The L Word*
We'd watch on her bed her flat stomach up and down with
    breath My lungs full every time
we touched and I almost drowned when she said "we are on
    two different pages"
and I ugly-cried for hours drinking gin in my ex-boyfriend's
    basement

The fifth time I kissed a girl was in the middle of a crowd
    during the Portugal Day feast
I told her to cut her hair She said "we should move in
    together" For two years we made out
and up on Brooklyn rooftops and Long Branch boardwalks
    until too many days came
and went of Mãe not looking at me Pai mourning the person I
    wasn't yet We kissed
for the last time before I moved into Tania's attic high on
    Xanax pug by my side

The sixth seventh and eighth times I kissed girls whose names
    I can't remember
The bar loud My temples throbbed My hands on their waists
    Their mouths wind tunnels
Heart silly putty and I got so hammered I walked Hot Goth Girl
    to the subway after we ate
shitty Jamaican patties then sat lost at the corner of Hudson
    and Grove
By that time the eggs were cold the toast was gone my
    mother refused to make more coffee

The last time I kissed a girl I was waiting for salvation in the
    form of jazz and fado
It was hot hard raining and I learned tanto tanto from the
    museum of her body—
that love is an art you curate with grief and not a choice like
    the Oxford comma She remains
every Whitney song from *The Bodyguard* We married in
    secret and everything is
except this love: aubade and war cry rolling on the shore of
    for now / for here / forever

Baby Steps (An Ars Poetica)

This is the first line, where I compare fucking you
to being swallowed by a wave so blue it's another planet,
and so big—McNamara surfing Praia do Norte big.

Then I cross out ~~fucking,~~ call it "making love" instead because
you've softened every edge of my tongue. Still, I am ballsy.
I follow with a list of sexy images: the sun a mango in the sky,

your hand a butter knife over the spread of my legs,
our pink mouths two schoolgirls running toward anything pink.
Public bathrooms as private islands, breath like cartoon birds

circling the hare knocked out by the turtle. I extend this
    metaphor,
talk about how our fate rides on this turtle's back, that if we
    have faith,
we'll get somewhere. The key: go slow. Baby steps.

I change gears though, contradict everything I said about the
    turtle to tell you
my favorite place in the world is now your back seat. I use
    lines like
"not fast enough" and "bedtime feels a lifetime without you."
    Heavy alliteration

follows, nonsensically: "not knowing anything newer, memory
    making
mincemeat of me, feeling all the freaking feels." Then comes
    the line
where I say how scared I am. Then the line about how scared
    you are.

"Wild Horses" plays on the radio, wild horses gallop across
    the page,
a fire burns in your father's village. I talk about silence, how we
    are
kindling to kerosene. In this end line, neither of us are sorry.

Morning Song

Driving home from the Stop & Shop, you glance over
at the Clorox and pretzels and get the urge
to wrap yourself around a pole

like a snake, like a stripper,
like an SUV yearning
for the hot crush of metal.

Holding her as she coos
like a bird seeing the ocean
for the first time, a part of you

wants to tear yourself to pieces,
pluck feather by feather.
Sitting at your desk

looking out the window
you think how close the planes get
to the top of buildings in this city,

you remember the last time you flew,
the last time you faked an orgasm,
the last time you rode like a ghost

in the wind—you rode like the wind
only to make sure every part of you was still
there, in that moment.

When there is a shooting
in an elementary school,
you drop to your knees, thank God it wasn't

her or her classroom. You run
to the bathroom and throw up,
you throw your hands up in the air.

Google "statistics of school shootings in New Jersey."
Google "where can I buy a gun fast."
Google "post postpartum depression."

What the Water Gave Me

after Frida Kahlo's 1938 painting

The name where everyone forgets
the *n* or adds another *a*
making me Maria or Mariana
or any other immigrant's daughter
or "where boats live" or "of the sea"
The ephemera of my grandfather
spools needles and tins of thread
crisply folded bills that shine
like emeralds in bathwater
The twins' reflection once tinted
steel against the buzzing skyline
the Dairy Queens and bodega kings
looking for loose change on the Riverbank
The dresses that never made me
the woman my mother hoped for
the birds never returned to Avó's cage
the respite from dark woods after dark-hearted
men took what they never asked for
All the lovers I buried with beautiful lamentations
All the siblings I drowned and the one I couldn't
All the seahorses carrying my daughters' dreams
All the carnations blooming from my wife's palm
At the foot of this claw-footed haven
blood red toes like black holes at the center
of a galaxy dazzling with fire and ice
I dizzy in my own becoming

Estou a sentir só este momento

like the nothing of a wave rolling ice blue
over sun-fucked sand and wet, wet shell,
like nothing in the way wind transfers verses
against blades, lullabying ashes and dust

of erosion and drones; nothing like
the hooked breath of old books, pretty
words wailing in the hand of another ear
before the line breaks and they fall deep

into the sound a cephalopod makes
when our legs become their legs and we wrap
neck, waist, and wrist, tangle into the bare
thread spread of land nowhere immeasurable,

a space between born and supermarket line
of lives we crossed through (eight billion bodies)
to find each other and did And a daffodil sighed
olive fields sung the whole world wept

A bird of spun gold with freshly plucked
leaf in mouth, smooth as the way this nothing
feels, the slow burn of your belly across mine
in moan, infinitely cavernous in polite conversation

If I Weren't This Body

or in this body part of this body and what parts of this body
make it my body why does this body love your body the way
bodies do when they touch other bodies whose bodies belong
to each other this body taught to love boy bodies hairy bodies
bearded bodies abusive bodies but this body also wanted soft
bodies breasted bodies perfumed bodies girl bodies now this
body queries its own body is it man body is it woman body what
makes it either and does it matter to anybody what kind of body
we embody and who body does this impact a lady body a bard
body a body of water a wetland a body of art a masterpiece
a body of bullseye a target some days a boulder body other
days barely a body bare and breathing a shiny body like a star
like a moon-filtered body like a magazine body or Instagram
model this body a lion this body a lamb a bad day body a sober
body survivor body medicated body hard-bodied hostage body
heavy body heavenly body pussy-bodied mama-bodied a can-
dle of a body a cage of a body eucalyptus tree of a body thimble
of a body fiction of a body fado of a body looking for another
body to believe it more than a gendered body will some body

II

You do not have to be good.

—Mary Oliver

Tanto Tanto

Last night I dreamt Oliver's wild geese
were arrows pointing toward
the pink-blue horizon I wrestled with

in my youth. Each *ave* indicating
aqui,   *aqui,*   *e ali*
are pockets of air ready to be filled

with everything we are capable of.
Mounting red mares, taming them
with the tightening of our teeth.

Emptying rivers so that where
a child thirsts, we cool their palms.
Taking pictures of posies,

lavender, poinsettia, and dill,
seeing Lorde's face in each one.
Breaking rock open like pomegranate

to find the lost scriptures of Rich,
Gibson, Winehouse, and Hurston.
There are so many ways I can learn

to take my coffee if you make it.
So many gorgeous ways
a bear can sleep.

Lines

You figuratively toe an invisible line in the metaphorical sand
say *D'aqui não passo* I won't do X say Y believe Z
I do it too Shut my eyes while my mouth's wide open to blare
    IMOs
convince you that even if you can't see it I always mean it
And not a day goes by that we are not oil and water piano and
    pedestrian
potato potato In this exciting new battlefield of memes and
    quarrels
I discover telephone lines deliver the most fucked-up messages
that your mouth can spit fire and put it out at the same time
There is nothing worse than drawing lines particularly when
we are so desperate to cross them I'll keep this in mind from
    now on
the way *andorinhas* muscle-memory between Lisbon and Porto
Maybe silence can build a footbridge from my bad nature to
    your good sense
Maybe it can say everything I want to but never do

Pussy in Space

It's been 22 days since my pussy floated out in space, spinning among supernovas who'll see many elections before they burn out, 528 hours since she's touched down on earth, and by earth I mean my partner's mouth, and by mouth I mean her tremendous tongue, which is a galaxy of its own, with blue moons and dwarf planets and auburn asteroids bouldering through and to the G-spot, which is a man's word for clitoris, which is a woman's word for freedom, and last night, while swimming through the creamy outer layers of a Pluto laced in black and flannel, my pussy lamented the almost-month of no orgasm, bloody tears dotting the Turkey Hill in my bowl, a rocket man floating in the distance, humming to her anchorless howling

Love during Retrograde

I.

heart under   house arrest

      the rest   of this   body back

road   roaming   like

      a doe   on the wrong side

of   mourning

      painting flowers   with its   tongue

so they will   never die

II.

in the morning,
robins place bets:
which kid will spill
the oatmeal, which one
of us'll yell "no yelling,"
which witch on Netflix
will make thump
upstairs, those unruly
jazz ghosts
dust bunnies
papers apologizing,
crayons quitting

III.

while Mercury tricks our eye
into believing she is backtracking

here I am double-booking
here I am last-minuting

here I am filling applications
for the imaginary

four-legged family member
no one agreed to

IV.

you got me the most magnificent
monthiversary card it got me
all weepy, wondering how
a straight man can write
such thick, lazy love
over the page like fog

V.

did I mention the fog? thick, lazy fog that goes on across space?
mantle over any sign of stars and the goats in my dreams
who sing fados to the rivers? last night I saw nothing out my
    window
and in my sleep one of them called "lover, lover, *volta, volta*"

Telling Another Story

After the spark and deluge of last night,
I open the window.

I hang my sheet like a prayer flag.
I tick the morning by, nails against mug.

I remember how we met a little differently;
both at opposite ends of an olive field,

debaixo da lua cheia, deliberately stepping
toward one another, wind lasso at our waist.

Upon meeting, you ask, "where have you been?"
I tell you "writing this life."

You say, "this is the end of that,
this is the beginning of this."

And so, a new story. A bouquet
of black-eyed poppies. The crossroad

church at Ferry and Wilson.
O céu de Lisboa, de andorinhas.

A body on break at the table,
a mind at rest without meds.

A ball and chain of feathers and gems.
Telling another story *em novo idioma*:

trust conjugated in the present and future
indicative. A bible in whale's tongue.

Two women holding hands: *oração*.
Two children joining them: *família*.

When My Mother Tells Me I'll Always Be a Loser

my heart jumps out through my mouth
and hauls ass toward your heart

pumping like a Newark boom box
a fired cannon red as fuck

dark as menstrual blood Your heart
will hug my heart hard as hell

tell it "Baby, it will be OK It'll be fine
Remember amor, our mothers

inherited their cruelty and I got
so so so SO much love to fill

that hole inside you she keeps stuffing
with sawdust" My heart will nod,

blue but wiping away thick tears
the liver mistakes for rain My heart

will tell your heart she's always wanted
a white picket fence but didn't know it

Brunch

Where I really wished we were:
the Antelope Valley Poppy Reserve,

a *sentir só este momento* amid
blood orange. Petals and petals

smeared and stuck to our body
like stains so that we are more

work than artist. I chug my mimosa,
slide my black boot toward your

brown flat, say "You're gorgeous, bae"
so loud I scare the birds, warn you

I'll probably still be hungry after this.
You always know what this means.

Capela da Nossa Senhora dos Aflitos

Here on this side of the ocean, dawn
swirls its face on morning waves, the mist

a mantle of woolen smoke around the cliff
so many women have jumped from. I walk steadily

to the old chapel *Nazarenas* pray in
for the return of their husbands, but I'm not

here to pray. Just stand and bear witness
to the crumbling blue and white tiles that form

the Blessed Mother of the Afflicted, the saint
of those plagued by fear and famine, phantasms

of the body and mind. No one knows I'm here
to consider sanity, to imagine a world

where illegal is not a person but an act,
on an Earth being swallowed by itself.

To the kneeling tourists on my left, I am nothing
more than an overwhelmed *Americana*

who forgot her camera but doesn't care. It looks
like rain is coming, and that is one less thing to wet.

On that side of the ocean, you tell me about the sweltering
heat of midafternoon Newark: "It's murder out here.

The sparrows stick to the cherry blossoms to stay cool.
And we all know how they love to fly, so imagine."

While Six Planets Retrograde, I Consider Mandalas and America

after Delia Quigley's "Fear" from her Divine Mandalas

I'm too American and not American enough to know what a mandala is, how it could be useful. My immigrant family taught me that if something has no real use, it isn't really real. And if mandalas are just symbols for the Universe, how do they pay a water bill, put meat on plates, keep children from orphanages of steel? What can a dreamer who knows dreams are circus clowns do with a search for the self? How do I find myself in the midst of chaos, looking for answers to all the questions: will fascism reign another four years? Will we be deepfaked to death, will black lives ever matter, will we trans humanity? Can a mandala help at all?

How do I explain the practicality of art to my late grandmother, who didn't come to America to raise no artist; didn't leave mother and siblings behind in a village buttoned by olive fields to work as a maid at the Ramada, freeze meat in plastic bags, to walk me to and from catechism, learn "good morny" and "bye-bye" for the mailman and teacher aids, to cook *cozido* and boil hot dogs, all for me to talk about mandalas, much less my pride in first-generationism, to shout off the rooftops of a page that no human is illegal, to write poems in the two languages she was *analfabeta* in?

How do I explain the energy of mandalas in a prayer to my dead grandfather, who didn't come to America to raise no socialist, for there was nothing he believed in more than the American Dream; who saved time, money, and bathwater to tailor suits for up-and-coming second-generation studs, hung Reagan calendars on humming refrigerators in hopes his money and

Hollywood machismo would trickle down to his son, uncle who went from owning a mechanic's shop to wearing a MAGA hat and pretending his niece wasn't always the kind of woman who scare men like him, the kind who knows capitalism and patriarchy are the root of all evil?

How do I convince my father of the power of mandalas, my father who didn't come to America to raise no queer, didn't leave his father's fields and tractor and shadow of his brothers' white-collars, his soccer buddies and hitchhiking youth to work construction in grimy Tri-state cities under Local 472, a proud union man who paid for both his daughters' colleges without ever owing a credit card, who tells me all people are equal and should live their truth unless those truths hurt people like him, to raise a daughter who knew better than to marry a man, who knew better and married a woman.

How do I tell my mother that a mandala I saw in Morristown reminded me of being her child, my mother who didn't come to America to raise no feminist, who dropped out of East Side at 15 because white folks taught her to fear books and black girls, who worked at Pitas Bakery and Lucy's Hair Fashion and dealt with a mother who didn't know how to mother, enabled a husband who didn't know how to be a husband, raised two children who didn't know that she didn't know but always blamed her for not knowing, who drowned her sorrows in telenovelas, only to have a daughter who teaches her kids that most important thing is to know "you don't have to be good" to be good.

And I'm sure there's a mandala out there for all of them: fierce lines, bold spheres, and light waves exploding in possibility. There are divine mandalas abounding in electric blue, menstrual red, the thick yellow of August that can center me while Mercury, Jupiter, Saturn, Uranus, Neptune, and little Pluto retrograde and show Avó and Avô, Mãe e Pai, that although I am not the woman they came to America for, I am the American woman fighting alongside immigrants like them. Because the most beautiful mandala is not the one teeming with a geometry everyone recognizes, but the one that places you inside a dialect for resistance, that reminds you an image is its own tongue.

Pussy Cleans the Bathroom

After an argument with my partner, Pussy Windexes down the mirrors, admiring how full her lips get before her period. Tackles the cold toilet next, a mermaid breaking through waves of depression and fatigue in search of other mer-pussies who have also not had sex in two weeks, who also blame Mercury's retrograde for their bae's inability to fuck after a fight, who also wish for Warren as president even though they feel The Bern. Finally, Pussy scrubs the tub with the same vigor as she rubs herself when she bathes alone, showerhead beating face, teeth grit in expectation, fingers between clit like cheerleaders waiting for the touchdown, my partner pounding on the other side of the door, demanding if she's almost done. Pussy throws her head back and shouts, "I'm coming Goddamnit, I'm coming!"

III

Love, we are both shorelines
a left country.

—Audre Lorde

Tanto Tanto

come to me
open boneless
and full-bodied

like the octopus
I dreamt we waited for
while the sun set

octopuses live fast
and die young
can we

use all three of our hearts
be as pragmatic
as blue-blooded

did you know the female
makes love
like we do

eager and always
with the threat
of cannibalism

before I scare you
with any more
cephalopod facts

come to me
like the final tide
like the moon is full

of more light
than our bodies
can hold

Ten Things I Never Told the Homophobic Portuguese Woman on Ferry Street

1. In this revolution, a dick is as useful as a knife in a soup bowl.
2. Our kind prides itself on *filhos educados*. Were you sick the day your mother taught silence is golden? Did she talk too fast when she said, "if you have nothing nice to say, don't say anything at all?" Are you proud of being *malcriada*?
3. I'd bet my month's salary that you are still heartbroken over never kissing Adelaide by the lake, summer of '74.
4. It must be nice to don the armor of heterosexuality. Do you take it off at night before bed? Is it temperature regulated? Is it bulletproof? If I throw a bag of dicks at it, will it break?
5. Speaking of dicks, I do have one. Purple, clean, safe, and always ready in my *armario* drawer.
6. May your children inherit only your temerity and never your cruelty.
7. *Vai pró caralho.*
8. Bae makes me cum the way an *onda* breaks during *bandeira vermelha*. I'm sorry you'll never know this life at sea.
9. I pray that your husband never leaves you for another woman. Or another man. But if he does the latter, you can't scream at him what you did at me. You're going to have to tell him the pussy is missing. And if that's the case, take your own advice.
10. When Amália sang "Estranha Forma de Vida," she was talking about us.

Oracular

Space: the final frontier! But
they've never seen the world we built

outside this place. This oracular planet
of dayglow orchids that bud and blossom and scatter

into seeds that bud, blossom, and scatter, auburn
oceans that gather and fill, roll and break

with glittery anemone, golden guppy, brave blowfish,
and the greatest great whites—

all strings of an aquatic hallelujah.
On our planet, chipmunks in drag paint Kahloesque

masterpieces, winged elephants in suits write sonnets
about their feet because no one gives a fuck

about size and weight and fame, and all we own
is our body, here a parable, a pulse;

praise the space we take up, you and me and our
daughters dancing to the synth and psalm of twilight.

Our citizens love like zombie lions,
so ferocious no matter what some Martian

might say about their carnation fetishes,
how animals that large will eventually forget.

They two-step like God herself
stomped down on the rainbow and made

mountain and commandment, tells us
we are the ones they've been waiting for—

a family of magical matter, mutating muscle
into wild eucalyptus and bloodlight,

where future generations will constellate,
where transbirds bury time beneath them.

Apology to the Snails I Crushed in My Youth

I inherited cruelty—
the sordid belief that to be big
is to break something smaller.
Avó's garden: the town square;
my fat little fist: a mighty guillotine
over your soft bodies; the sun:
a magnifying glass
of good intentions

In the mornings
I trek over gendered rituals
with tired tentacles, smile
at the swat of sadness;
crack at my kids' screamy demands
for gentle brushing and more milk;
I come apart at the cruelty
of silence against sleep

Last night,
I told my family: be grateful
home is wherever
we carry our hearts. Simone clapped
her chubby hands together and said,
"God, what are we using our story for?"
How super—to be small
and believe in bigger things

The Quiet

Sometimes I can't stop you
from leaving. Some conversations
require silence as punctuation,
demand solitude right after.

For the best. So that the best
can eventually resurface
on our fingertips like wildfire,
spread all the good that's left

over each other's shoulders,
backs, thighs: unfillable wells.
Sometimes, in this quiet,
I am both in and out.

Sometimes the quiet between
no longer and not yet
opens me up like evening primrose,
and I trace your footsteps

down the stairs and out the door,
over the weedy sidewalk to where
your car is humming with hesitation.
Sometimes I take the quiet

to listen. Listen to the moon's
lax moan, the crack of kitchen light,
the cricket's tired mutiny
against every child's cry.

The oven's uprising. The backdraft
that follows. The certain leap from
the steady cliff. The phone's frugal
fado. The apologies of doors.

New Hope

"Are ducks racist?"
I asked,
hunched over the pier.
"They seem to
stick to their kind,"
you say.
"Are ducks gay?"
I asked
your silence.
"Of course," you said.
"Why wouldn't they be
both?"
In fact, you're sure
ducks are us:
simpleminded
complex as fuck;
we watched them
in the water
come together
and apart
always in their feelings.
And that is how we said
"Yes"
to that moment.

Ode to My Pussy

For doing it alone, with no help
from the head and arms and legs
that hung inert between contractions
but ticked and spun and wept

every night in hopes that you could
shoulder the hurt, carry the burden,
pull the most supernatural beings
I'd ever see out of me.

For falling in love and staying there
despite all the unruly fools you let in
with and without permission. The sad
souls you pushed out with no remorse.

For finding the wildest iris,
a bloom that envelops you with sunlight
from a childhood adventure, that swells
the way an octopus does before eating.

If I never do anything right again,
if I never rid myself of the barbed wire
around my brain, I'll always remember
that I have you, the holy holy tide.

Scar

like an almost moon
or smile
or almost smiling moon

I watch this mark
of you still here
roll and rise

ever so slightly
with every sigh
your eyes kneeling

into the air
as I trace it slow
without touch

you worry it'll
look unsightly
this reminder

of working holy
cells and nerves,
muscles and bones,

skin and heart—
unscathed and absolutely
beautiful

cut
I curl into
by night

Hum for Impending Ice Storm

We ready with coats,
hats, scarves, and mittens
to brave a cold window
someone left open.
Bodies bundled and stitched

together in an order
I find in zippers and hemlines,
reminded it takes decades
before anyone can invent
something as powerful as thread,
as precious as an apron.

The wind sweeps the children
into the car. I drive with one hand
on the wheel, one hand
on a stainless-steel mug,
eyes peeled back
by caffeine and traffic.

I've stopped asking for things
I want. I only ask for what I need:
a love that won't sour,
a mess I don't clean,
a job I won't tire of,
art for art's sake.

When things always got here,
to the impending ice storm,
I always pulled myself back
onto the majestic dusk

of Nazaré, the silver singing
off the backs of dead
sardines, but last night,

last night I was there,
and it was very dark,
and I wasn't anything more
than my resilience.
With the right filter, though,
I was still having
a good time.

Fado for My Last Love

Had I followed my foremothers' manual,
I would have already ironed and hung
your clothes, stocked the fridge fully with meat and cheese,
stored your favorite deodorant in bulk on the bottom

of our linen closet. I'd watch news on my laptop
and let you have the living room, leave you
to your rom-coms and *Grey's Anatomy*.
But I burned that handbook way back

in middle school, used the ashes
for my first tattoo. In this life, I will never be
a proper Portuguese wife.
Only the wolf with a compass for a heart,

the smile by a well peeling an orange.
What you are marrying is an odd cutter
of cucumbers; a load starter-and-leave-it-
overnighter; hairpins in the corners of the sofa;

and I guarantee I will lose your other sock
every time. I'll fill our Netflix queue
with horrible horror movies, your ears
with so much rambling during a documentary

you'll seek refuge in our basement,
next to the clean underwear and bath towels
you put to wash, you fold perfectly.
What you are committing to is a lifetime

of "what's for dinner no I don't want that"
and my crying at the drop of a dime
when I think of Rocky and Adrian,
this wallflower you will always drag

to the dance floor to sweat your moves, this
imperfect lover with fireworks for pelvic bones,
this sandwich-eater who loves your sandwiches
the way white girls do the Jonas Brothers,

this poet who is all rainbow and inside the lines
when you find me with your mouth,
saddle and slide until I am all glitter and verb,
this pug-lover who will flood your feed with

pug memes in hopes you'll one day change
your mind about dogs, and I pray this be enough—
the badly cut salad and haphazard hamper,
the tired steam engine pulling into your station,

this nightstand full of books and empty bottles,
this fado we call ours, this coming-of-love,
our very own manual, and if so, I vow
to never give up on us the way the couple

in *The Notebook* didn't, I vow to point out
how problematic this movie is every time
you watch it, vow to always find a solution
to our problems, to fight instead of flight,

love you in all the ways our grandmothers
never could their lovers. I vow to write it all
down for when I am no longer
a moment but a memoir.

IV

We are the ones we have been waiting for.

—June Jordan

Tanto Tanto

The pink and pomegranate peonies remind me
of your petal-print button-up, my favorite
shirt of yours, but I don't announce it.
Maria da Graça is not the kind of woman

who appreciates my ritual running of hands
around your collar and down your chest every time
you wear it. Instead I tell her that just because
they blossomed into a bushel of stars

last year does not mean it'll happen again.
She strokes the soil where the peonies were,
tells me: "*Tem fé!* See the small green tears?
That's proof." So I consider buds and proof,

what the planter sows into the planted.
How me of little faith imagines the forced flora
springing up any day now, considers carrying
a bouquet down an aisle without flinch or doubt.

The dirt path we beat to get such fertile ground.
I leave my mother to horticulture and faith.
Remember to water these fucking things, I tell myself.
Remember to buy her more flowered shirts.

The Body

I envy your faith in the body,
in its ability to cope, heal, suffer
the battles biology/ecology/man
wage against it. A bellyache,
a bitten tongue, a black eye.

Alzheimer's. Cancer. GHB. God
only gives you a cross heavy enough
to bear, but He never considered
how hard the straw is on the camel,
what it's survived. A woman's body—

what you deem insurance against
hurricanes, viruses, racism, and divorce
even after watching Gloria Steinem
interview a Congolese woman
burned and raped by twenty men

ten years ago. "She lived," you said,
but what does her body house now
but the banshees of youth, cataracts
that see through things, planets
of scars, a blood-pumping grenade,

an ache so viscous and vicious, so wide,
the Great Flood becomes a shower.
In spite of every prayer I fake,
despite how much Steinem says otherwise,
our bodies (more often than not)

are a forgotten *aldeia*: a bloodstained
skirt on the line, a lover's dirty boots
at the door, children chanting rhymes
about cats, a steaming pot of soup
on the stove, humming . . . humming . . .

To Know Saudade in America

Ten years ago, I wrote "Saudade," an ode to first-generation
    Down Neck kids.
There are old apartments, noisy sewers, and bodega candy in
    it, rose water and a lady
cursing in Portuguese down Market Street. A doll commits
    suicide in it. This poem
smells like iron and tracks, first-period blood. I fall in love with
    this poem, send it
to *Awesome Journal, Cool New Lit Mag. The Paris Review* and
    New Yorker, too.
None of them publish it.

Two years ago, *Poetry* published a white dude's "Saudade." I
    imagine the man
able-bodied and small-mouthed, a self-proclaimed coffee
    snob, passing on
the garbage Starbucks calls espresso. His coffee is Meltino,
    served by a Brazilian
as exotic as his travel stories, hair vines down her back, brown
    and glistening
from the sun that flushes his foreign skin in a quaint cafe in
    the "nice" part of Rio.
His saudade, unpronounceable

but "real" enough for print, was reposted on Facebook and
    Twitter, becomes
the "Poem-a-Day" my students proudly forward me. Tonight, I
    wear a dress
I bought for funerals I've never attended. The sleeves stir with
    the whirring
of the desk fan like the one in the Gentleman's Shop basement
    where my Avô

steamed suits he tailored for the bodega kings. This dress
    never fit me the way
he made everything fit.

I tell myself grief can't swallow you whole, only in parts, so I
    have time to consider
how many bees still exist, how many more luxury lofts will go
    up before anyone
remembers rivers are breathing things. I think of fresh mint
    and chicken soup,
an old house and no shoes, low tides and lost rings, pine trees
    and bent pages.
An immense olive field.

Don't tell me what saudade is, or that you know it.
Ask me instead what names I have for "gone,"
what comes back to itself without fleeing first.

Sometimes the Bird Sometimes the Hunter Sometimes Both

Forgive me for that left hook,
that shot below the belt I didn't mean
what I said and if I did, I shouldn't
Be wary of me, but know my neurons
have always been woodpeckers My heart
line a river of seedy tributaries

✖ ✖ ✖

You are so good at never being wrong;
an ace at making me 2007 Britney
and when I grab the reins of Something You Can't Control,
I dream of biting the thumb off the Okay emoji
you passive aggressively text "This is normal"
my therapist says "Great, we're normal," I chirp

✖ ✖ ✖

One day we will make it through one week
without a trigger ("what's for dinner") or
a subtweet ("look how full the moon is")
We will drive down 78 after the fight,
in the rearview will be an open lane, will be
resentment in the form of 1000 singing crows

Savage Beauty

after Lee McQueen

In the interstitial room of morning we wake more animal than
    anything;
holes and lids, fur and folds pinned, tucked, and ruched to form
the perfect functioning beast at the desk in the cubicle behind
    the wall
against the window at the top of the highest building we
    unjump from.
By night we feral back, ferry horned hearts into ribbed nests
    waiting
to witness the most magnificent thing in the world flutter from
the eye socket of the full moon. We need such savage beauty:
monarchs and murmurations, swallows creasing against orchids,
carnations twirling cigarettes, snapdragons with Swiss army knives,
marigolds and magnolias nippling the breasts of unseen gods,
bloody roses and blood-red rosaries. I was raised to pray
for beautiful things. Feathered, daggered, and dangerous
replacements for mothers on days where we leave
the house not in our body but in a bag of mewling kittens
like the one my grandfather buried before the mother cat
    could tell.

Pussy Writes Horror

The protagonist is a thirtysomething queer femme artist whose partner goes away for the weekend to a work conference in Philadelphia, and she is left alone to masturbate for the next seventy hours to terrible lesbian threesome videos, only to discover the vibrator's battery has run out and the wire on the charger is as frayed as her nerves, so she drives to CVS, only to step out and trip on the worn entrance carpet and dislocates her arm, the good arm, the dominant hand arm, the masturbating arm. An ambulance is called and seven hours later, Pussy is back home, in a cast, unable to love herself in the dirty, divine way she planned to, confident that this is some high-level Stephen King shit—for what can be worse than three days in solitary celibacy. "It's been 7 hours and 15 days," she sings, bald and sad as Sinéad in the nineties.

Pansy

Like women like sun
radiant & resplendent

Like body—hybrid
woodland & home

Like alive & brimming
with spotted possibility

Like queen, ruler
of unhinged kingdom

Like a *pensar morreu*
um burro & I am no ass

V

You and I are always going to fight for love.

—Andrea Gibson

Tanto Tanto

Joy like the pit of a dusty peach
inside the dark when you drum
on the steering wheel in traffic,

when my leg crosses over yours
in a sleepy wave, when finches fly
from your mouth like psalms.

I'm impossibly full but still ravenous
at the thought of your palm
grazing against my thigh

like a two-day-old balloon
making its way across the yard to the child
ready for every pop and pull.

Wild, hungry joy finds me finding
every way to laud a universe
that always provides

but that you only praise
when my soft fists become
the treehouse your father never built.

Irreparable Harm

*Family separation causes irreparable harm: It has short-term
health implications and changes in bodily function, behavior,
and working memory.*
　　—Dr. Julie M. Linton

*no one puts their children in a boat
unless the water is safer than land.*
　　—Warsan Shire

At the border
a child cries like
a burning poppy
a bleeding lamb
an axe to redwood

"This signals trauma," says a pediatrician from Texas
This gets a "womp womp" from a Trump staffer
This carries a serenade across oiled rivers

At the detention camp
a child inside a cage
recites her multiplication tables
hums a Selena Gomez song
whispers the prayer Abuela taught her

This: 1 times 1 is 1
This: "hmm hmm hmm back to you"
This: Santa María, Madre de Dios,
Amén Amén Amén

　　✗　✗　✗

I watch an officer thumb   through his phone on Ferry
watch cars   stop go   stop go   on Market
a cat cross Adams   with the confidence   of a white man
watch a blade cut   what is expected   to grow back

there's no harm in tuning out   she tells me   "self-care
     is important"
but what   when you care   too little   or too much
where in this city   is it safe   on this spectrum
is it safe   to exist   where is it safe   to exist

     ✗ ✗ ✗

I do not hide this world from my daughters
Sugarcoating is for strawberries, and like
all my foremothers, I forewarn
that outside this kitchen, there is more dark
than light That children like them but not them
are hungry in all the ways one can be
Girls like them but not them
are wrangled and raped in all the ways
a girl has been Out there, kids like them
but not them sleep on concrete,
on dirt, under tin and rain
When the baby refuses dinner,
I remind her of little ones in favelas
who would kill for her carrots
When the oldest throws a tantrum
I tell her that her dolls have more clothes
than Appalachian children
That every crumb and thread
on their plates and sweaters
are god and gold
God and gold

     ✗ ✗ ✗

My grandmother never shouldered the burden
of grandchildren poached at the border

of LaGuardia when she landed
in what a family friend asserted

was the country that gave and gave
until it had nothing else to give.

My grandmother taught "be wary of an open hand—
it'll close sooner or later"

When a hand opens and invites you in,
there is irreparable harm

when it clenches, passes your body on
to someone else.

Like I'm Already Dead

Like I'm already dead—a carnation in a dim funeral parlor, corpse stiff in burgundy Sit your knees on the little stool, rest your head on my stuffed belly Tell me again how your favorite day in the history of the world is June 30th Describe how hot-hard the rain slammed against our car that night, how hot-hard our first kiss made us Tell me how you first said *I love you* by accident, how I didn't shave until you returned from Portugal that summer That even at my most, I am still the one your soul loves
Hold my hand in the hush

Like I'm already ash—the shit gray of pines after fires ravaged most of Bairro Alto Tell me about your day at work, how the office was a circus tent, how the administration fails the teachers and teachers fail the students and students fail each other and everyone goes home anxious and unable to do anything but sit in front of a screen for hours swiping and waiting to do it all again tomorrow Tell me you're over the moon having married someone who cares tanto tanto in the face of fierce American apathy Sing me your affection

Like I'm already a ghost—at the top of the stairs, hands soft as silk, bare feet on the too-cool floor, humming a fado closer to hymn Burst through the door and slip the fat silver ring you gave me years ago onto my barely-there finger, close the curtains we just bought Accept my apology and call night by some other name: darkbulb or expiredlight Remind me that dinosaurs never became extinct but phantasms, their bones aide-mémoires of what love wore 70 million years ago
Open-mouth laugh till you're dead too

On the Last Night of Pride

The owner of the oldest girl bar in NYC
shakes her ass outside in a stupor
while bodies speckled with rainbow
glitter, stringed things, pins, and nipples
walk by, while bodies in dark blue
lean cross-armed against guardrails
blocking off streets to control
the drunk nude gays, keep them from mixing
with other Villagers walking dogs,
leaving work, making a milk run.
Allegedly, a patron steals an officer's hat
and Bar Owner busts inside with her bouncer,
commands Sunday Night DJ to "turn this shit down
NOW," orders every lady in the place
with style and grace to give up
the stolen hat or at least the person
who swiped it. Someone sick of the shouting
tells her "What if they're not here?"
and a gale of accusations and threats
and an almost-altercation has my body spinning
in defense of one queer from another.
In this America, I am an ex-smoker who
smokes weed but wants a cigarette, an alcoholic
craving Fireball but kissing her fiancée instead.
My club soda is warm, I am already tired
of this decade, of law trumping love
in the lesbian bar. Drake becomes
a mosquito buzz circling these bodies
still made for target practice, these bodies still
policed and unsung, these bodies dancing anyway.

Poem Where I Try Not to Think about My Partner's Existential Crisis

I finally learned how to make breakfast eggs
my way, sunny-side fried and oblong,
without a recipe or some made-up memory
of my mother gently cracking one perfectly
against the rim of the hot pan and grabbing
my hand to scramble They are not perfect
but my partner says, "they're so good babe" And I am proud
and I feel like a good woman who's earned her keep
I imagine feeling this way every day of my life
I completely ignore what this says about me

I witness a murmuration on the way to work, swarm
of black against the gravel and burnt green
of winter lawns, and damn if this is not a metaphor
for queerness, for how we never touch down for fear
of taking up space, for how everyone looks in panic,
questions why we are there, what we are doing—
can't we just fly off or at least try to fucking blend in
the birds peck at imaginary meals
the guy behind me honks and says "Bitch!"
I mutter back "your mama" like I'm in fifth grade

My grandmother had no dolls to play with growing up,
save for her youngest sister held against her small
bosom and pretend nursed until her mother came back
from the fields My children have so many dolls
most of them with hair tangled by negligence,
limbs bent in imagination; I want to give them the joy
Disney says they deserve, all the laughter extinguished
in my throat when I was their age My grandmother drew
a voodoo doll on paper When I became a mother
I became a voodoo doll, deliberate and unafraid

I sage the house and set crystals by the window
to charge under the new moon; labradorite,
amethyst, and tourmaline wait like soldiers
for a signal, hoping they clear away the darkness
my antidepressant can't, conscious of how American I am
in this moment, appropriating indigenous practices
I know nothing of; I was raised on weeping saints
and inherited guilt and all I want is a goddamn break
All I want is to secure a bag All I want are more
than suggestions of life in my living room

Hard

When the blackbirds land
on the front yard
looking for bread,

watch your daughters,
watch them
from the window.

Their fascination
at the Guinea-fowl tulip.
The wave of their hands

like a cast spell. Watch
the blackbirds disperse,
away from the borders

white supremacy builds.
Watch your daughters
watching from the window;

know Hell is other people
and we are blackbirds
from no-man's-land.

An Abecedarian of Gratitude

All the ways I am always thankful for this queer life, this odd
Beast of days filled with art and music and housework and
Children raised compassionately, intelligently, as close to
Dangerous to the patriarchy as possible. Grateful for the
Early morning whirl of dental care and caffeine, lunchboxes
Filled with fresh fruit, packaged cheese, and yogurts,
Going bad if we don't eat them this week, the combing of
Hair tangled by family folklore and bizarre dreams
In which she is heroine in the woods, where the wolf is more
Jester than assassin, and none of the apples are poisonous but
Kept in beaded ice baskets, shiny and all for the taking.
Looking out the window, I carefully bite one of the banana
Muffins you made last night, remember a time when
Nothing was this simple, this thought-out and thoughtful, this
Organized tenderness that leads me out the door strong-armed
      with joy,
Prepared for a world constantly policing, insulting, and instigating,
Querying our faces and bodies and moods and minds
Rallying in the name of a Jesus more like me than they can
See and nothing else matters when work is done and I pull up
To our driveway, climb out with kids, books, and grocery bags,
Umbrellas trembling with wet, the October clouds heavy and
Vanishing behind me as I kick off my coat, kiss you quickly,
Warm my hands at the stove, shimmying elated to see
"You made canja," my favorite, the oil and chicken stock starlight
Zooming through planets of pasta and thinly chopped carrot.

Your Pussy

A bowl of cold strawberries
on the sill.

I think about this
quite often.

My greed over your every
freckle and follicle,

knuckle deep
in Love.

Now I know hunger:
a bird, humming and whet.

I am terrified of being
this happy.

Sonnet for This Queer Body

Hail the double take of white men when I walk past,
head bald and big-earringed, smear of incandescent
pomegranate over my pout. Praise the mom-pouch
poking over the faux leather painted on my legs,
the "Ohs!" grandmas emit when I make way for them
in the supermarket. Compliments to the claws
painted black and pink, gold-ringed hands that write
poems to a world always extending itself beyond reach.
Pay tribute to the tattooed arms like pirate flags,
the radical nose springing forth like alien bloom.
Salute these sagging tits and coiffed cunt, these misty
eyes cursing those who can't see such fucking divinity.

All we have are our love

And our guts, baby.

—Bitch and Animal

Tanto Tanto

You waited for me to look up when the mayor was reading our
vows, but I knew if I did, I would melt into a puddle of idont-
knowwhat like in old cartoons, or laugh uncontrollably like the
meme of the office guy falling off his chair, but when I did, our
eyes were fixed, our hands steady, our bodies there and almost
stone and I thought, it's all happening like in *Almost Famous*.
But I'm not Penny and you're not William; this isn't a movie—it's
so much better including our soundtrack and I never thought
I'd marry, much less wear red to my wedding. But I'm a poet and
I'm going to say that red was the perfect choice—the color of
revolution in carnations, in fire and blood and everything that
will always keep me happy. I'm so happy we happened I couldn't
even sleep remembering that Monday night in 2014 when you
read a love poem you don't remember writing but I remember
saying to myself "I hope she finds someone to love her tanto
tanto and completely the way she loves that someone back"
and holy shit, HOLY SHIT. You did. I do.

Notes

"Tanto Tanto"

Tanto means "so much" in Portuguese.

"Autobiography of a Fufa"

Fufa is a Portuguese derogatory term for a lesbian or queer woman.

"*Estou a sentir so este momento*"

The title is taken from a line from Santos e Pecadores's song "Fala-me de Amor"; it means "I am only feeling this moment."

"Lines"

Andorinhas means swallow.

"*Capela da Nossa Senhora dos Aflitos*"

The title is named for the chapel located in Nazaré, Portugal.

"While Six Planets Retrograde, I Consider Mandalas and America"

Delia Quigley's "Fear" is from her installation Divine Mandalas: Your Journey Within. More information can be found on that at https://deliaquigley.com/2019/04/22/mystics-and-mandalas/.

"Ten Things I Never Told the Homophobic Portuguese Woman on Ferry Street"

Bandeira vermelha means red flag in Portuguese and is usually displayed when the ocean is not suitable for swimming.

"New Hope"

The title is named for a small quaint town in Pennsylvania.

"Irreparable Harm"

The epigraph from Dr. Julie M. Linton comes from the following article: Tanya Basu, "The 'Irreparable Harm' of Ripping Immigrant Kids from their Parents," *Daily Beast,* June 20, 2018, https://www.thedailybeast.com/the-irreparable-harm-of-ripping-immigrant-kids-from-their-parents-6.

Acknowledgments

My gratitude to the journals, magazines, and anthologies who published the following poems in this book, some in earlier versions:

Cahoodaloodaling: "Morning Song"

DMQ Review: "Sometimes the Bird Sometimes the Hunter Sometimes Both"

The Harpoon Review: "The Body"

Journal of New Jersey Poets: "Irreparable Harm," "Like I'm Already Dead"

Luna Luna: "Baby Steps (An Ars Poetica)," "Tanto Tanto" (*come to me*), "Tanto Tanto" (*Joy like the pit of a dusty peach*), "When My Mother Tells Me I'll Always Be A Loser"

OyeDrum: "Your Pussy"

Platform Review: "Fado for My Last Love"

Queen Mob's Teahouse: "Autobiography of A Fufa," "Lines," "The Quiet," "Savage Beauty," "While Six Planets Retrograde, I Consider Mandalas and America"

Wildness Journal: "What the Water Gave Me"

"Your Pussy" was published in *The Impossible Beast: Queer Erotic Poems* (Damaged Goods Press, 2020).

SHOUT-OUTS

To Amalia and Simone, I love you tanto tanto.

To the CavanKerry Press team—thank you for giving this queer love story a most special home and treating it with the care it yearns for.

To Dimitri Reyes—this book would not be here without you, hermano. Gracias por your careful eye and extraordinary heart.

To my parents, sister, and family who never waiver in their support—Amo-vos muito.

To my Write On Poetry Babes: Lynne McEniry, Kathleen Kremins, Ysabel Y. Gonzalez, Tamara Zbrizher, paulA neves, Grisel Acosta, and Claudia Cortese—your sisterhood sustains me and I hope to write alongside y'all forever ever.

To my besties Emiley, Liz, and Tina, my GFB fam, all my Divine Feminists, Rutgers MFA homies, and all my dear friends—your love is tremendous and appreciated.

To Ananda Lima, Grisel Acosta, and Darla Himeles—super poets! Thank you for your loving words on the back of this book.

To my Poetry Queens Mary Oliver, Rachel McKibbens, Adrienne Rich, Audre Lorde, Staceyann Chin, Ellen Bass, Bitch, June Jordan, and Andrea Gibson—this book is a product of all your legacies.

To all LBTQ+ children of immigrants—we are worthy and beautiful; may we love fiercely in face of the fight.

To Cindy Laura—this is our Notebook.

To you, Reader—tanto, tanto amor.

CavanKerry's Mission

A not-for-profit literary press serving art and community, CavanKerry is committed to expanding the reach of poetry and other fine literature to a general readership by publishing works that explore the emotional and psychological landscapes of everyday life, and to bringing that art to the underserved where they live, work, and receive services.

Other Books in the Florenz Eisman Memorial Series

Tanto Tanto has been set in FreightSans Pro, the sans serif counterpart to the typeface FreightText. The humanist forms of FreightSans Pro give it a warm and friendly appearance. It was designed by Joshua Darden and published by GarageFonts in 2009.